PRE-READER

Hop, Bunny!

Explore the Forest

Susan B. Neuman

NATIONAL GEOGRAPHIC

Washington, D.C.

Vocabulary Tree

FOREST

ANIMALS

bunny
deer
squirrel
bug
snake
turkey

PLANTS

tree
leaf
fern
flower

WATER

pond
stream
waterfall

bunny

Hop, bunny!

In the forest

a bunny can see many things.

Hop, hop, hop!

Big trees stand tall.

trees

Others lie down.

There are leaves and ferns.

leaves

ferns

flowers

There are tiny flowers.

Hop, hop, hop.

Deer dance through the woods.

red deer

Squirrels scamper.

red squirrel

praying mantis

Bugs are busy.

grass snake

Snakes slither.

Wild turkeys trot.

wild turkeys

stream

Bunnies hop by ponds, streams,

waterfall

pond

and waterfalls in the forest.

Hop, hop, hop!

YOUR TURN!

Tell a story about a bunny.
Pick one picture in each row.
Then tell your story.

WHAT PLANTS DOES IT SEE?

WHAT ANIMALS DOES IT SEE?

WHAT WATER DOES IT SEE?

Trade paperback ISBN: 978-1-4263-1739-2
Reinforced library edition ISBN: 978-1-4263-1740-8

Book design by David M. Seager

Photo Credits

Cover, Andy Rouse/naturepl.com; 1, Michael Hamrah/Flickr/Getty Images; 2–3, amana images RF/Getty Images; 4–5, Rèmy Courseaux/Biosphoto; 6–7, M. Watson/ARDEA; 8, Stephen Dalton/Minden Pictures; 9, Alan Kearney/The Image Bank/Getty Images; 10, Bill Hatcher/National Geographic Creative; 11, Ocean/Corbis; 12–13, Arterra Picture Library/Alamy; 14–15, Alex Saberi/National Geographic Creative; 16, Elliott Neep/FLPA/Minden Pictures; 17, Kim Taylor/npl/Minden Pictures; 18, Fabio Pupin/FLPA/Minden Pictures; 19, Gerry Ellis/Minden Pictures; 20–21, Ron and Patty Thomas Photography/E+/Getty Images; 22, Andy Rouse/naturepl.com; 23 (UPLE), Stephen Dalton/Minden Pictures; 23 (UP CTR), Alan Kearney/The Image Bank/Getty Images; 23 (UPRT), Ocean/Corbis; 23 (CTR LE), Alex Saberi/National Geographic Creative; 23 (CTR), Gerry Ellis/Minden Pictures; 23 (CTR RT), Elliott Neep/FLPA/Minden Pictures; 23 (LOLE), Bill Hatcher/National Geographic Creative; 23 (LORT), Ron and Patty Thomas Photography/E+/Getty Images; 24, blickwinkel/Alamy

National Geographic supports K–12 educators with ELA Common Core Resources.
Visit natgeoed.org/commoncore for more information.